John P. (John Prescott) Whitney

Whitney's Florida Pathfinder

For the Tourist and Invalid

John P. (John Prescott) Whitney

Whitney's Florida Pathfinder
For the Tourist and Invalid

ISBN/EAN: 9783337194734

Printed in Europe, USA, Canada, Australia, Japan

Cover: Foto ©Lupo / pixelio.de

More available books at **www.hansebooks.com**

WHITNEY'S

FLORIDA PATHFINDER

FOR THE TOURIST AND INVALID.

GIVING LATE AND RELIABLE INFORMATION OF THE
VARIOUS ROUTES BY LAND AND WATER;
THE CONNECTIONS; THE POINTS
OF INTEREST; HOTELS,
ETC.

ARRANGED AND PUBLISHED BY

JOHN P. WHITNEY.

FOR THE SEASON OF 1874-75.

ISSUED FROM PATHFINDER OFFICE,
66 JOHN ST., N. Y.

HOME
Insurance Company of New York,

OFFICE, No. 135 BROADWAY.

Abstract of the Forty-Second Semi-Annual Statement,

Showing the condition of the Company on the first day of JULY, 1874.

CASH CAPITAL,	$2,500,000 00
Reserve for Re-Insurance,	1,919,971 53
Reserve for Unpaid Losses & Dividends,	243,238 83
Net Surplus,	549,171 04
TOTAL ASSETS,	**$5,212,381 40**

Summary of Assets.

Cash in Bank,	$387,821 27
Bonds and Mortgages, being first lien on Real Estate, worth $5,321,000,	1,989,330 41
United States Stocks (market value),	2,092,125 00
State and City Bonds, " "	58,500 00
Bank Stocks, " "	134,753 00
Loans on Stocks, payable on demand (market value of Securities, $432,285.00),	315,050 00
Interest due on 1st July, 1874,	60,273 10
Balance in hand of Agents,	144,314 65
Bills Receivable,	16,091 50
Premiums due and uncollected on Policies issued at this Office,	14,122 47
TOTAL,	**$5,212,381 40**

Liabilities.

Claims for Losses outstanding on 1st July, 1874,	$241,623 83
Dividends unpaid,	1,615 00
TOTAL,	**$243,238 83**

J. H. WASHBURN,
Secretary.
THOS. B. GREENE,
C. K. FRANCIS,
Ass't Sec's.

CHAS. J. MARTIN,
President.
A. F. WILLMARTH,
Vice-Pres.
D. A. HEALD,
2d Vice-Pres.

PREFACE.

The continual increase of travel to Florida of invalids and pleasure seekers, and the eager search for information concerning the various routes which convey one to this Italy of America, have led us to compile and publish this much needed Guide.

We have endeavored to obtain the latest and most reliable information concerning the schedules of the various routes by land and water. We have extended to each route sufficient space to fully set forth the same.

We give in brief, the points of interest on the St. John's river; including the principal Hotels, also the several Mineral Springs of note.

We briefly notice the dates of the landing of the different expeditions, on the Atlantic and Gulf coasts.

The schedules of the various routes, have been obtained from the managers of the same; though possibly, later changes have been effected to extend additional accommodation.

For the convenience of tourists and others, we present a list comprising the principal hotels to be met with, in the leading cities, in connection with a trip to Florida.

There are many things that we are obliged to omit for want of space ; and we trust our readers will cheerfully overlook this fault, as in other respects, we have carried out our desires successfully.

Florida.

Nearly all are acquainted with the facts concerning the landing in Florida, of the veteran cavalier, Ponce de Leon, while in search of the spring, whose waters he expected would give him a new lease of youth and vigor. Why, even at the present day thousands are hunting out, visiting and drinking the waters of the one-thousand-and-one Mineral Springs to be found throughout the United States ; and with no less anticipations than those of this veteran.

It was on the 3d day of April, in 1512, that Ponce de Leon first put foot on Florida, near the present site of St. Augustine ; and the day being Palm Sunday—in Spanish, *Pascua Florida*—and meeting on every hand an abundance of wild flowers, he gave to the land the name of FLORIDA. The Indian name is said to have been Cautio. The banner of the cross was planted, and the country therefore considered by their Catholic Majesties a Spanish Province. And what assumption ! Suppose that these ill-used natives —the Indians—had, in turn, visited old Spain, and unfurling their standard to the breeze, claimed Spain as their own by right of discovery, what would have been the effect ? However, the existing intelligence of 1512 was sufficient guarantee of Spanish possession ; and civilization went marching on.

After searching about for two months, and becoming disgusted with the natives, and not finding any gold—or even the Fountain of Youth,—the adventurers departed.

A second time this veteran visited Florida, but with no better success. He soon returned to Porto Rico, and carried with him a mortal wound, received in conflict with the Indians, which very soon caused his death. The discovery and landing upon the coast by this veteran, opened the way for others, who soon after followed, and made the coasts of Florida resound with the death-cries of the white man and the Indian.

During the past few years the climate and surroundings of Eastern Florida have attracted extensive attention, and where hundreds formerly visited this State for health and pleasure, thousands now visit it and make it their winter home.

Florida has received its highest praises from American tourists and travelers, who have passed months in health-restoring climates abroad.

For the consumptive individual—if the visit is accomplished before the disease destroys the foundation for its re-building—and for the business man whose brain and nervous system are worn down with business over-exertions and care, there is no better medicine, for relief and cure, than the pure air and sunshine of this Italy of America.

And to those, whose sports lead them to the Forest and to the Stream, there is no other state in the Union that extends greater opportunities.

It is quite surprising to note the agreeable change that comes over one while enjoying the climate and the surrounding attractions of Florida. How readily one will cast aside business cares and vexations. Under such atmospherical influences the invalid gradually increases in health and strength, and the over-worked mind of the commercial man steadily recovers its former healthfulness.

Expeditions to Florida.

History records the landing, in the New World, of Christopher Columbus, in 1492, and five years after, in 1497, Sebastian Cabot, sailing under the English flag, coasted the shores of the southern states. In 1512, Ponce de Leon landed on the coast of Florida, just north of the present site of St. Augustine. Diego Miruelo, in 1516, visited the coast. In 1517, Fernandez de Cordova reached the shore, and soon after, one Anton de Alaminos, visited the coast; and again in 1521 Ponce de Leon made his second voyage. Panfilo de Narvaez, in 1528, visited the Gulf coast. In 1539, De Soto landed with his followers on the Gulf coast; and in 1545, a treasure ship from New Mexico to Spain was wrecked on the eastern coast. The four Franciscan Brothers landed on the Gulf coast in 1549. About three years after, a whole Spanish fleet, excepting one vessel, was wrecked on the Gulf coast. In 1559, Don Tristan de Luna visited the Gulf coast.

In 1562, the French Protestants, or Huguenots, under John Ribaut, arrived on the coast, near the present site of St. Augustine. Sailing north, he landed at the mouth of the St. John's river, and erected a landmark. Continuing north, he landed at Port Royal, and endeavored to establish a colony. In 1564, Rene de Laudonniere, arrived at the present site of St. Augustine ; after examining the harbor, he sailed for the St. John's river, and built a fort where Ribaut had previously landed.

In August 28, 1565, John Ribaut, (who had previously returned to France,) again appeared on the coast and landed at St. John's Bluff. In the same month and year, Menendez, whose mission was to exterminate the Huguenots, arrived at and founded St. Augustine, (1565.) Sailing north, to the mouth of the St. John's river, he drove off the French fleet of John Ribaut, and returned to St. Augustine. He at once set out by land to attack the Fort at St. John's Bluff—held by Laudonniere. Arriving early in the morning, he attacked the fort and massacred the inmates. Laudonniere, with a few others, escaped. Over the mangled remains of the French was placed this inscription :— "We do this not as unto Frenchmen, but as unto heretics." On Menendez's return to St. Augustine, a solemn mass was celebrated and a Te Deum sung in commemoration of the victory.

A severe storm overtook the fleet of John Ribaut, and all were cast upon the shore at Matanzas, only to be butchered by Menendez, in squads of ten, with their hands pinioned behind their backs. Thus nearly three hundred men met death, by putting faith in the promise of this noble leader. (?)

In 1567, Dominic de De Gourgues, a Huguenot gentleman arrived on the coast, and, with aid from the Indians, fully avenged the wickedness perpetrated by Menendez, and over the lifeless bodies of the Spanish, he wrote : — "Not because they are Spaniards, but because they are traitors, robbers and murderers."

5

St. Augustine was plundered and burned by the English under Sir Francis Drake, in 1586. In 1611, and 1638, it was pillaged by the Indians. In 1665, the town was plundered by the pirate, Capt. John Davis; and in 1681 was again attacked by the Indians.

Gov. Moore, of South Carolina, in 1702, captured the town, but was unsuccessful in attacking the fort. Before he withdrew he burned the town. In 1710, Gen. Oglethorpe laid siege to the town. He planted his guns on Anastasia Island, behind the large sand hills, on the North beach, and, after an unsuccessful attempt of forty days to capture the fort, he withdrew.

In 1763, Spain ceded Florida to Great Britain, and three years after it again passed over to Spain. In 1819, Florida passed into the hands of the United States. The change of flags in East Florida took place at St. Augustine 10th of July 1821, and Territorial Government was established in 1822. Florida was admitted as a state into the Union, in 1845.

Increase of Travel.

Since the close of the war, the travel to Florida has steadily increased. The following are the estimates for the past five years, from the season of 1869-70 to May 1, 1874 : —

About 4000 tourists visited the state during the winter of 1869-70.

During the season of 1870-71, about 7000 invalids and tourists visited the state.

The following season, 1871-2, the travel increased to about 14,000 visitors.

The winter season of 1872-3, there were over 20,000 visitors in the state.

In the panic season of 1873-4, about 25,000 invalids and tourists visited Florida.

Fernandina

Fernandina is a fine old town, built by the Spaniards. It has a population of about 3000, which support seven

There is a fine shell road, which leads to the hard ocean beach, which presents a fine drive of over twenty miles. The city has a telegraph office. Fernandina is reached by rail from Jacksonville. Also the steamers "Dictator," and "City Point," of the "outside" route to Charleston, and the steamer "Lizzie Baker" of the "inside" route to and from Savannah, make regular stops during their trips each way.

Jacksonville.

Jacksonville is the commercial metropolis of Florida, and, we might further remark, the entrance gate of over one half of the entire travel to the state. It is here that the invalid stranger and the veteran Florida sojourner rest awhile from the fatigues of their journey.

Jacksonville is an enterprising and prosperous city ; the present population is about 14,000. The city is situated on the St. John's river, about 25 miles from the ocean. The city is named in honor of General Audrew Jackson. Bay street is the commercial thoroughfare, it being nearly a mile in length. The commerce of the city is extensive, and the merchants are enterprising and liberal. Leading out of the city is a fine hard shell road, which presents a delightful drive of over two miles in distance. Fine turnouts may be procured at the several well equipped livery stables.

An enormous business is the cutting and shipping of the Florida Pine ; frequently the river is dotted with foreign and home vessels awaiting their turn to be supplied. The banking facilities are offered by the first National Bank of Florida, and Ambler's Bank. The city possesses telegraphic facilities to all parts of the United States. Steamers for all points on the St. John's river leave Jacksonville every morning. (See hotels, routes and their connections.)

St. John's River.

This grand sheet of water is created by the overflow of the numerous springs and swamps in the southern portion of the state ; it flows, unlike any other river in the United States, directly north for nearly four hundred miles, when turning abruptly, to the east, it empties into the Atlantic ocean. Many portions of the river are six miles wide, and north of Lake George no part is less than one mile in width; at Palatka the river becomes narrower.

There is a charm attached to the incidents of a trip upon this sheet of water—apparently a succession of lakes—that one will not soon forget, especially when contrasted with the cold bleak winds of a winter trip upon the Hudson.

Points and Distances on the River.

Giving the distances from Jacksonville. Sailing south is termed going UP the river. The points marked with an asterisk are on the right going up.

Mulberry Grove,*	- 12 Miles.	Beecher, - -	101 Miles.
Mandarin, - - -	15 "	Mt. Royal - -	113 "
Hibernia,* - -	23 "	Georgetown, -	123 "
Magnolia,* - -	28 "	Volusia, - -	144 "
Green Cove Sprgs,*	30 "	Orange Bluff, -	147 "
Picolata, - - -	44 "	Hawkinsville,*	174 "
Tocoi, - - - -	49 "	Cabbage Bluff,	175 "
Federal Point, -	58 "	Blue Spring, -	180 "
Orange Mills, -	63 "	Sanford, - -	204 "
Palatka,* - - -	75 "	Mellonville, -	205 "
Welaka, - - -	100 "	Enterprise, -	211 "

For information regarding accommodations at the above localities; see hotels on the St. John's river.

The Principal Springs.

Among the many attractions which the State presents to the tourist, the mineral springs form no small part. We briefly present the name and location of the principal ones. The first in order is the Sulphur spring, at Green Cove Spring Clay Co. It is about 35 feet deep, and discharges about 2000 gallons per minute. Fine facilities are afforded for bathing. It is said to have effected many wonderful cures.

Orange spring, Marion Co., is situated on Orange Creek, which empties into the Oclawaha river.

The celebrated Silver spring, in Marion Co., is on the Oclawaha river. During the season, steamers from Palatka convey parties up this river, which is nearly two hundred and fifty miles in length. Silver spring, in the same county as above, is on Lake George.

Blue spring, Volusia Co., a few miles north of Enterprise, on the east bank of the St. John's, is probably the largest in the state. It forms a wide river of itself. One can readily observe the movements of the shoals of fish below, which pay no attention to the visitors looking down upon them.

Green spring, at Enterprise, is about 80 feet in diameter, and is said to be fully 100 feet deep.

On the western shore of Lake Jessup, there are several large sulphur springs. Boats drawing over three feet of water cannot enter this lake.

In the centre of the St. John's river, toward Lake Harney, there boils up a tremendous spring. It has been sounded to the depth of nearly 300 feet and no foundation touched.

Ponce de Leon spring, St. John's Co., located on the new settlement of Ravenswood, just west of St. Augustine, is used for its health-giving properties.

Boiling Ocean spring is at the eastern part of Anastasia Island, just north of Matanzas Inlet.

Points of Interest on the River.

Having left Jacksonville, the first point of attraction on the river is Mandarin, a village of about 150 inhabitants. It is one of the oldest settlements on the river. It was once the scene of a fearful Indian massacre; during the Indian wars, the Seminoles fell upon it and massacred all within its limits. There are boarding house accommodations, Post office facilities, etc. Here located is the winter residence of Mrs. Harriet Beecher Stowe; it is the dark cottage on the left of the pier and is almost obscured by the foliage of the large oak and other trees.

Hibernia is a pleasant resort located upon an island on the opposite bank of the river. It is quite a resort.

Magnolia is one of the most pleasant resorts to be found on the St. John's. It has good hotel accommodation. Black creek is located but a short distance to the north of this point. During the winter season, a small steamer navigates the stream as far as Middleburg.

Green Cove Spring is located two miles south of the above point; one of the most extensively patronized resorts on the river. The Sulphur spring is one of the attractions at this point; the temperature of the water is about 75 degrees, and is as clear as crystal. The sulphurous condition of this spring is quite distinguishable by taste and ordor. Green Cove Spring extends excellent accommodations.

Picolata is 14 miles from the previous point, located on the opposite shore. It is the site of an ancient Spanish settlement, the evidence of which is long since destroyed. Opposite Picolata, on the west bank, are the remains of fort Poppa, an old earthwork fort, built during the Spanish era. Before the completion of the St. John's wooden tramway, in 1871-2, Picolata presented quite a lively appearance, when all passengers, for St. Augustine, were here transferred and conveyed across the country by stage. Five miles south of this point the steamer halts at Tocoi.

At Tocoi, visitors are transferred for St. Augustine. During the summer of 1874, the road was re-laid with modern iron T rails; first-class rolling stock procured, and trains complete the trip, a distance of 14 miles, in about thirty five minutes.

Palatka is the largest town on the river, south of Jacksonville. It has a population of about 1500 inhabitants. The town is nearly one half mile in extent; and does an extensive trade with a flourishing back country. It possesses postal and telegraphic facilities, churches, etc. The *Eastern Herald*, a weekly paper, is published here. Just south of Rollestown, an old English settlement, is the entrance to Dunn's lake. Palatka is the terminus of the steamers "Dictator" and "City Point," of the Charleston (outside) line ; also the steamer "Lizzie Baker," of the Savannah (inside) line. It is also the terminus of the St. John's river steamer "Florence," which leaves Jacksonville every morning, returning the same day. Passengers are here transferred for Enterprise, Mellonville and the Oclawaha river. During the Winter season, small steamers make the trip from Palatka to Dunn's lake; also excursions to the celebrated Silver spring, on the Oclawaha river. This river is celebrated for its wild and picturesque scenery. Near the spring is the site of an old Indian village. Leaving Palatka, the great beauty of the upper portion of the river becomes apparent. It was appropriately named by the Indians, Welaka— a chain of Lakes. The principal lakes are Lake George and Lake Monroe.

Immediately opposite Palatka on the east bank is the orange grove owned by Col. H. L. Hart, consisting of 700 trees, some forty years old, which yield an income of from $ 12,000 to $ 15,000.

San Matteo is a thriving settlement located five miles south of Palatka on the same side of the river. It possesses Post office and hotel accommodation.

Welaka is twenty-five miles above Palatka, opposite the entrance of the Oclawaha river. It is the site of an old Indian and Spanish settlement. South of Welaka the river widens and forms Little lake George; gradually expanding, it forms Lake George, which is ten miles wide and eighteen miles in length. One of the largest orange groves on the river is located upon Rembert island in this lake.

Volusia is the site of an ancient Spanish settlement, all trace of which has long since been destroyed. During the Indian wars a log fort was here constructed. The present village was settled in 1818.

Enterprise is situated on the north bank of lake Monroe and is the terminus of the Palatka steamers. Mellonville and Sanford are on the opposite shore of this lake. During the winter season, small steamers ply from Enterprise through lake Harney on the route to Salt Lake, and which is the nearest point to the Indian river from the St. John's; fishing and hunting parties are conveyed to lakes Jessup and Harney by small steamers. Lake Jessup is quite shallow; boats drawing over three feet of water cannot enter the lake. At Enterprise, parties are furnished with conveyance to reach New Smyrna and the Indian River. From St. Augustine frequent excursions are made in yachts to the Indian river, which is the sportsman's paradise for game, fish, etc.

Mellonville is located on the south bank of lake Monroe. It is the site of fort Mellon, erected during the Indian wars. In the vicinity of Mellonville there are several fine orange groves. Hotel and boarding house accommodation, etc.

New Smyrna is located upon Indian River, near Mosquito inlet; about 22 miles from Enterprise, and 65 miles south of St. Augustine. In 1767, Andrew Turnbull arrived at the coast with his colony of 1500 Minorcans and established the above settlement; and in consideration of his wife being a native of Smyrna, Asia, he gave the same name to his new settlement. Large crops of indigo were cultivated, which proved quite profitable to Mr. Turnbull. The Florida indigo commanded the highest price of any sold in the English market. In 1772, there were 40,000 pounds exported. The colonists remained under Turnbull until 1776, when, not being treated according to contract, they left the settlement and located at St. Augustine. At New Smyrna visitors are accommodated at private houses. The Indian River truly is the Sportsman's paradise; the river is alive with innumerable varieties of fish, and the forest is abundantly supplied with game. The celebrated orange grove owned by Capt. Dummitt is here located, south of the inlet.

St. Augustine.

St. Augustine, the oldest town in the United States, is situated in a direct line, about 33 miles south of Jacksonville. It is 350 miles north from the southern point of Florida, and 14 miles from the St. John's river.

The population is 2000. It has five churches, good schools, telegraphic facilities, and there are also two newspapers published, the *Examiner*, established in 1858, Mathias R. Andreu, Proprietor ; and the *Florida Press*, established 1870, J. F. Whitney, Proprietor. The town is built upon the precise point that was occupied by Menendez. Its Indian name was Seloy. On the arrival of the

Spanish there were found habitations of considerable size, which had been built by the Indians. Geographically, it is somewhat similar to New York, or Manhattan Island ; being bounded on the north by the mainland and on the east by the North river, the Harbor entrance and the Matanzas river, with Anastasia Island forming the breakwater, and on the south and west by the St. Sebastian river. For the benefit of tourists we herewith present an original map of the city and its surroundings, which will give a good idea of the Bay and Ocean, including various landmarks.

On the arrival of the visitor from Tocoi, the first objects of attraction that greet the eye, are the substantial Bridge that spans the St. Sebastian river, and the long and narrow causeway which leads to the city.

We frequently recall the time when the steady arm of the ferryman brought us safely over this stream, and we stepped upon the muddy bank and wended our steps to this quiet nook of Augustine ; and how, previous to the completion of the St. John's tramway, we patiently awaited the welcome blast from Henry's stage horn, bringing that which could give us tidings, seemingly of another world.

Leaving the causeway in the rear, the visitor enters beneath the foliage of oak and other trees, with that never absent article—the moss— clinging in long skeins to the branches.

The residence on the right, with the fine surroundings, is the home of the senator—Hon. A. Gilbert, while upon the left is the residence and fine orange grove of Dr. A. Anderson ; and in the rear of the orange grove will be found the elegant mansion and grounds of Henry Ball, Esq., formerly the old Buckingham Smith place.

Emerging from out this archway, the tourist soon arrives ,in front of the "Plaza de la Constitution," and is then in the heart of the most antique city in America.

In 1870 the stages took their passengers at Picolata, and occupied about 7 hours in the journey over ; and on reaching the St. Sebastian river, where the bridge now stands, the coach was driven into a flat boat or scow, and by

13

Map of St. Augustine.

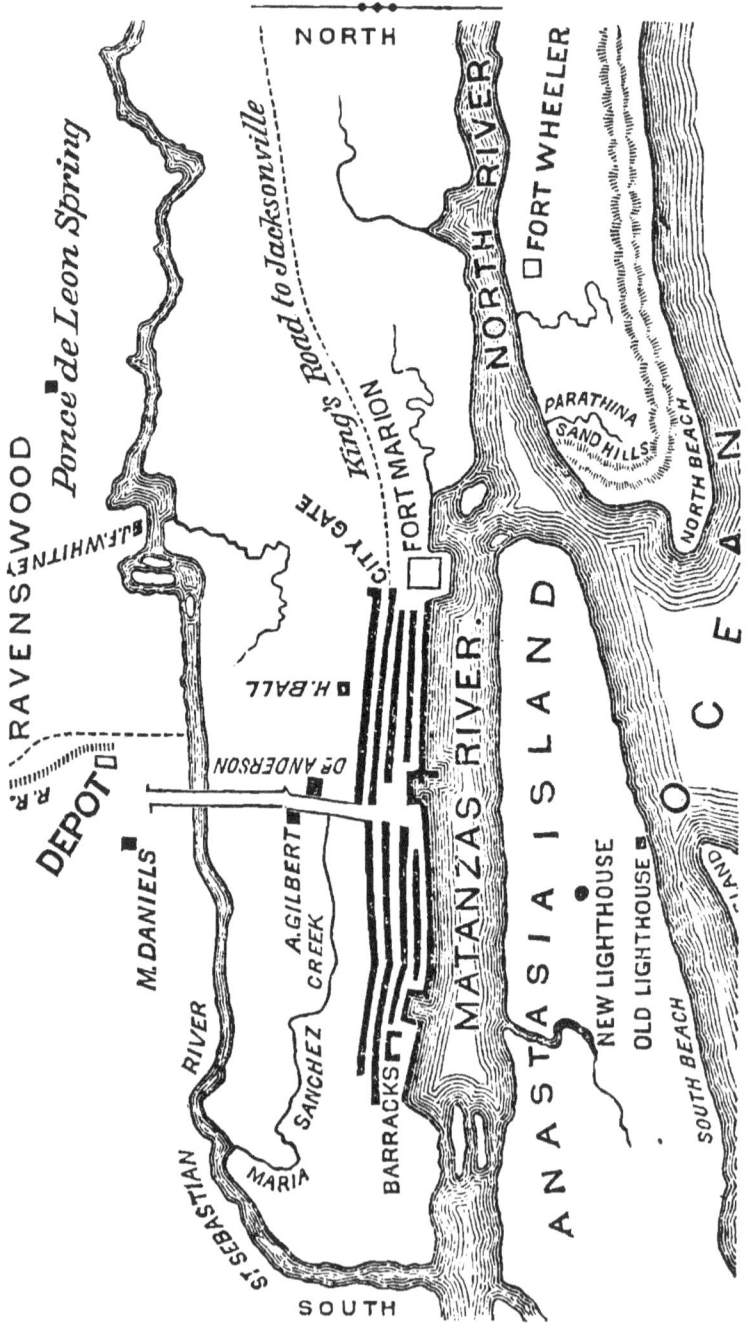

NORTH

Ponce de Leon Spring

RAVENSWOOD

J.F.WHITNEY

King's Road to Jacksonville

NORTH RIVER

FORT WHEELER

FORT MARION

CITY GATE

PARATHINA
SAND HILLS

NORTH BEACH

OCEAN

R.R.

DEPOT

M.DANIELS

H.BALL

DR ANDERSON

A.GILBERT

SANCHEZ CREEK

RIVER

ST SEBASTIAN

MARIA

BARRACKS

MATANZAS RIVER

ANASTASIA ISLAND

NEW LIGHTHOUSE

OLD LIGHTHOUSE

SOUTH BEACH

ISLAND

SOUTH

14

means of a rope drawn across the river. The ferry was under the charge of James Hartshorn, who resided near the same. John Henry introduced the present feature of blowing the horn before reaching the ferry, to notify the ferryman of his approach, as the time of arrival varied from sunset to midnight. Fifty cents was the toll for a stage, and five cents for a foot passenger. Step by step has St. Augustine progressed, until the present day, when the screech of the modern steam whistle fills the air.

Visitors to St. Augustine.

The estimated numbers of visitors in St. Augustine during the last five seasons, are as follows :—

In 1869–70, conveyed from Picolata by stage, about 400 visitors.

For the season of 1870–1, about 700 visitors came over from the St. John's river, by stage from Picolata.

In the winter season of 1871–2, on the opening of the St. John's tramway, about 2000 tourists visited St. Augustine.

The season following, 1872–3, about 4500 people visited the Ancient City. And during the season of 1873–4, upward of 6000 visited St. Augustine.

Winter Residences.

A large number of wealthy visitors from the North and other sections, having spent a winter in Florida, and becoming fascinated with the climate and its healthfulness, have purchased building plots in and about St. Augustine, and have erected elegant winter residences.

From the winter of 1870 to the winter season of 1874, no less than three hundred and fifty thousand dollars have been expended for the construction of these dwellings.

The Streets.

There are four principal or main streets which extend north and south. The first one passed, on entering the city, is Tolomato street, upon which is located the Catholic Cemetery. The second is St. George street, and is termed the Fifth Avenue of the city. The third, Charlotte

15

of the town. It is nearly a mile in length, and from 12 to 15 feet in width. All of these streets are quite narrow. The cross streets are much narrower. The fourth is Bay street, which commands a fine view of the St. Augustine Bay, Anastasia island and the Ocean.

All of the old Spanish residences are constructed of Coquina Rock—which is a conglomeration of small shell—found and quarried in large quantities on Anastasia Island. It is covered over with stucco, and afterward whitewashed.

Many of the houses, with high roofs and dormer windows, have over-hanging balconies, along their second stories, which seem, almost, to touch each other across the narrow street.

The principal streets were formerly paved or floored with shell concrete, portions of which can still be observed above the shifting sand, and heavy vehicles were not allowed to travel upon the same. There are great numbers of modern style residences, with elegant grounds, in and about the city which are well worth seeing.

King's road, which leads from the city gate to Jacksonville, was constructed in 1765 by subscription.

Fort Marion.

It stands at the north-east end of the town and commands the inlet from the sea. It is built of Coquina, and said to be the best preserved specimen in the world of the military architecture of its time. It is the oldest fortification on the Western continent. The original name was "San Juan de Pinos," the name being afterwards changed to "San Marco," which it bore, until the change of flags, in 1821, when it received its modern title of "Fort Marion."

It covers about one acre of ground and would accommodate a garrison of one thousand men, and one hundred guns. It was begun in 1520, and completed in 1756, the Indians being compelled to do the labor of building.

Over the entrance are the Spanish coat-of-arms, the name of the then Governor, the chief engineer of the works, and the date of the completion of the fort. Its walls and watch-towers remain intact, but its guns are dis-- mounted, and the moat is dry.

It is, in all respects, a Castle, built after the plan of those of the middle ages of Europe. There is the moat, which was flooded from the St. Sebastian, through the deep and broad fosse, which formerly connected with it. There are the inner and outer barriers, the barbican, the draw-bridge, portcullis, wicket, and all the appliances of such fortifications. It is what may be called, in modern military parlance, a four bastioned fort.

The inscription over the Gate, or Sally Port, of the Fort, is as follows :—

"Renando En Espanael Senr Don Fernando Sexto Y Sindo Govor Y Capn Gendefs C N Avcdelaf Y S V prov, Elmairscal De Campo D N Alonso Frnzdie Rediase conclavioestecs. To Ll oelan O. D. 1756, *Diriendo Las robrel Capyniero, D N Pedro De Brozas Y Garay."*

TRANSLATION.

Don Ferdinand the VI., being King of Spain, and the Field Marshal Don Alonzo Fernando Hereda being Governor and Captain General of this place, St. Augustine of Florida, and its province, this Fort was finished in the year 1756. The works were directed by the Captain Engineer, Don Pedro de Brazas Y Garay.

In Fairbanks history of Florida we find the following :— "In 1586, the Fort was constructed of the trunks of Pine trees, set upright as a Palisade, but without ditches. The platforms were of trees laid horizontally and filled in with earth ; but the works were in an unfinished state and not capable of a defense against a superior force. St Augustine when destroyed by Drake boasted of a Hall of Justice, a Parish Church, and a Monastery".

During the Seminole war, Osceola and Coacoochee, (or Wild Cat,) were captured by stratagem, and confined in the two apartments in the southwest angle of the fort.

While here confined, Coacoochee (or Wild Cat,) complained that the cell in which he was placed was too damp and affected his health ; whereupon, he was removed. Here an elevated seat, for the sitting of the court, afforded him the facility of reaching the grated window above, by means of one Indian mounting on the shoulders of another. On the evening previous to the night of his escape he remained an unusually long time on the ramparts of the fort, where he was allowed to walk daily, for exercise. He was called three times by the guard, before he obeyed the summons to come down. He had evidently been taking his observations of the manner in which the sentinels who guarded outside the fort were stationed, to enable him to determine the safest route to pursue, after he should escape from the window. This he effected, during that night, so noiselessly, that when the sentinel, who had paced the whole night before the door of his cell, was about to open the door, just at dawn, to examine, Osceola appeared at the grating of his cell, and with a smirk of delight exclaimed ; ''Wile Cat gone.'' When the sentinel opened the door, he saw nothing but the bare walls, and the narrow window through which the Indian had made his escape. Osceola was afterwards removed to Castle Pinckney, Charleston, where he died.

In 1836, the terra plain of the northeast bastion caved in, exposing a deep and dismal dungeon. We quote, from a lecture delivered by Dr. J. Hume Simons, at the fort, in St. Augustine, and afterward published in the *Florida Press*, of that city, the following :

''Impelled by curiosity, the U. S. military engineer, having charge of the repairs of the Fort and sea-wall, descended into this dungeon ; when, to his surprise, he discovered the skeleton of a human being manacled to the wall. He also discovered a strong wall, still further to the N. E. But what particularly excited his curiosity was the discovery of a broad stone, differing greatly in dimensions and appearance from those of which the wall was built. He noticed moreover that the cement which held this stone in its place differed in composition from that which held together the stones of the other parts of the wall, and appeared to be more recent. Whereupon, he ordered his masons to explore the mystery, by removing the stone; when the present dark, dismal, fearful dungeon was disclosed. But, oh horror of horrors! what else did he discover? Two iron cages suspended from hasps in the wall of the dungeon. One had partially fallen down, from rust and decay, and human bones lay scattered beneath it on the floor of the dungeon. The other remained in its position, holding a bundle of human bones. The latter may now be seen in the Smithsonian Institute, at Washington. The broken cage, with all the bones, except those which I hold in my hand, were buried in the sand-mound, to the north of the Fort. I recognize these as portions of the tibia and fibula (or leg-bones) of a female."

The fort is extensively visited during the day by strangers. Everything in and about the fort is kept scrupulously clean by the Sergeant of the same, Mr. McGuire, who takes pleasure in conducting visitors over the grounds, and telling them, in his own frank and interesting way, all that he knows regarding its history. The best hours to visit the fort are from 10 a. m. to 4 p. m.

Town Wall and Gate.

Regarding the wall, there are some doubts concerning the material of its construction. Whether it was composed of the same material as the old Fort, or was merely a rough stockade of pine logs, is a matter of conjecture.

If a stone wall ever existed there is not, at the present day, any evidence of it. Probably the material has been removed and at present forms a part of some old residence existing in the Ancient City. However, this wall or stockade is supposed to have been built some two hundred years ago, and served as a protection to the north end of the city against an attack from its enemies. It was situated on the south bank of the ditch.

The ditch, at the present day, is quite visible, and, at one time, it connected the moat-water around the Fort with the St. Sebastian river; but during the late war all evidence of this connection was destroyed by the construction of the present north-western embankment.

The only existing portion of this wall or stockade is the City Gate ; that being quite a picturesque and imposing relic. The ornamented lofty towers, the loop-holes and sentry boxes, are well preserved ; one can readily wile away the moments examining and studying this antique structure of defence.

The Sea Wall.

The sea-wall is nearly one mile in length ; connecting with the Fort it extends south below the Barracks, and serves as a protection to the entire bay-front of the city. There are two basins, the upper and the lower, which are used by the numerous yachts which sail the bay. The wall is built of Coquina, upon the top of which rest large slabs of Granite obtained at the North.

In 1690, it was found that the tide water was making encroachments upon the site of the Fort and Town, when, for their protection, a sea wall was begun at the Fort, and continued that year to the Plaza, and subsequently extended the full length of the town. The wall was repaired and cap-stones put on by the United States Government, during the years 1837 to 1842. Since that time it has received slight repairs.

The wall is about four feet wide, and affords a delightful promenade—especially on a moon-light evening. The stillness of the evening being broken by the continual roar of the Ocean surf greatly adds to the romance.

The Catholic Cathedral.

This structure is the largest and oldest house of worship existing in the town ; it was erected in 1793, at a cost of $16,650.

The quaint Moorish belfry, with its four bells, which are set within separate niches, together with the clock, form a complete cross. The peculiar chimes which these old relics of bells give forth, the odd surroundings of the belfry, and the antique interior of the Cathedral, make it one of the most interesting objects to be met with in the Ancient City.

Upon one of these bells appears the date 1682. This was taken from the ruins of the old Chapel outside the City Gate, in which several Priests were killed by the Indians, after' which, it was sacked and burned. Nothing but the foundation of the Chapel now exists. It was called "Nuestra Senora De La Leche," or "Our Lady of the Milk." The erection of this Chapel was the result of a superstition of the Spaniards, borrowed from the ancient Romans. "Our Lady Of The Milk" is simply the "Juno Pronuba" of the Romans, whom the Roman matrons invoked and implored, in her proper temple, to furnish them with a proper supply of *nursing* milk for their infants.

Among the interior decorations of the Cathedral, we may mention the following :

The niche for the image of St. Augustine is just above the High Altar, painted in azure, with gilt edgings ; inscribed above : "Sancte Augustine! Ora Pro Nobis." On the right of this, or to the east, is the niche for the Saint Aloysius ; inscribed : "Sancte Aloysi! Ora Pro Nobis." On the left, or to the west, is that for Saint Ambrosius ; inscribed : Sancte Ambrosi! Ora Pro Nobis."

Outside of the Chancel, to the west, is the altar dedicated to the Virgin, and, on the opposite side, to the east, that dedicated to Saint Joseph.

Yachting—Points to Visit.

No locality in the State presents a finer opportunity for yachting than the bay at St. Augustine. There are numerous fine yachts which convey parties to the many points of interest ; among which we would suggest a trip to the North beach ; the Sand hills, the locality where Genl. Oglethorpe planted his guns ; the South Beach ; a sail up North River, or a visit to Fish's Island ; the old and new light houses on Anastasia Island. The new light house is one hundred and sixty-five feet high from low water mark. The old light house was built more than a century ago. It will soon be mentioned as a relic of the past. The Coquina quarries are but a short distance from the light-houses. The formation of Coquina rock extends along the coast for one hundred miles.

A pleasure trip also is one to Matanzas, where there exists the ruins of a Fortress, which are supposed to be of more remote origin than any structure in the Ancient ·City.

St. Augustine is a favorite resort for members of the several yacht clubs of the North. During the winter season yacht racing and other sports are indulged in, and we venture to say that the day is not far distant when the snow-white sails of the yachts of the North will be filled by the gentle breezes on the Florida coast.

Ravenswood.

The visitor, upon leaving the Depot, passes over the Causeway and Bridge which lead to St. Augustine.

From the Bridge, looking up the river, on the left, will be observed the recently erected dwelling of John F. Whitney, Esq., the proprietor of the new projected settlement of Ravenswood.

This is the pioneer residence located upon this tract, comprising over one thousand acres, and designed by him as a new settlement. From its close proximity to St. Augustine, and its sloping, dry and healthful position, it promises to become a favorite location for northerners desirous of building-sites and Orange Groves in the immediate neighborhood of the Ancient City.

The prices and terms of sale may be obtained from J. F. Whitney, at the office of the *Florida Press* or, at his residence, on the settlement of Ravenswood.

St. Augustine Library.

This public Library was established during the season of 1873-4. It is located on the rear ground floor of the once Spanish Governor's Palace. Upon the tables are to be found files of the leading New York dailies, including numerous weekly publications; also works of fiction by well-known authors. During the winter season a register is kept open for entering visitors' names, which are published weekly in the *Florida Press*.

The Plaza.

The "Plaza de la Constitution," situated in the centre of the town, is surrounded by a neat rail fence, with seats arranged for the convenience of visitors; while encircling it are the Catholic Cathedral, the St. Augustine Hotel, the U.S. Court House, the Ancient Market, with its rude pillar supports, and other buildings of less importance.

During the early part of the Revolution, the effigies of John Hancock and Samuel Adams were burned here by the British troops.

Nearly in the centre of the Square stands the Monument erected in commemoration of the Spanish Liberal Constitution in 1812. Upon the east side of this Monument appears, in English, the name of the Square, while directly beneath, in Spanish—which, through the vandalism of wanton boys, has been partially effaced—appears the following:

Plaza de la Constitucion.

* * * * * *la en esta Ciudad de San Augustine de la Florida Oriental, en* 17 *de Octubre de* 1812,

Siendo Gobernador el * * * * *Don Sebastian* * * * *del orden de Santiago.*

Para eterna memoria El Ayunamento Constitucional Erigio Obeligio.

The following, in English, though by no means a translation, will give the idea supposed to be conveyed to the world by the above:

Just before the cession of Florida to the United States, the King of Spain granted a liberal charter to the citizens of St. Augustine and of Florida, and this Monument is a memorial erected by the Spanish citizens of St Augustine. The date of this Constitution was the 17th of October, 1812.

During the Winter Season, the Square is frequented by the *elite* and fashion of our Northern Cities, and through them St. Augustine—as is continually asserted in the leading publications throughout the country—has truly become the Newport of Florida.

The Barracks.

The above building is located at the southern extremity of the town, at the terminus of the sea-wall, and at present it is occupied by the U. S. Government troops.

The building was formerly used and designated as the St. Francis Monastery.

Spanish Governor's Residence.

The residence of the old time Spanish Governor is located on the corner of St. George and King Streets. It has undergone extensive repairs ; the south wing has been removed and an extension added to the rear. The high coquina wall that formerly edged on St. George and King Streets have been replaced by a neat wooden rail fence.

Convents.

The old St. Mary's Convent is quite an interesting building. It is located on St. George Street, just west of the Cathedral ; a portion of the ground floor is used as a store for the sale of views of the locality.

In the rear of St. Mary's Convent is a more recent building, formerly used by the Sisters of Mercy ; but at present it is used and designated as the Bishop's residence. The building is built of Coquina stone.

The Convent of the Sisters of St. Joseph, built during the summer of 1874, is located on St. George Street, south of the Plaza. It is also built of Coquina stone.

The Confederate Monument erected in 1871, in honor of their dead, is located on St. George Street, just south of Bridge Street.

Cemeteries.

The Military burying ground is located just south of the Barracks. Under three Pyramids are the ashes of Major Dade and 107 of his men, who were massacred at Fort Dade, in the western part of Sumter Co., by Osceola and his band.

. The Catholic burying ground is located on the northern end of Tolomato Street.

The Protestant burying ground is located on King's road, just north of the City Gate.

Churches.

The Presbyterian Church, with its adjoining Chapel and Sunday School room, is located on the south end of St. George street. Rev. C. O. Reynolds, Pastor.

The Episcopalian Church is a neat building, situated directly opposite the Cathedral, on the Plaza. Rev. Wm. Munford, Rector.

The Methodist Church is located on St. George street, north of the Plaza. Rev. Mr. Howard, Pastor.

The Baptist (colored) Church is situated on the outskirts, southwest of the city, and west of the Maria Sanchez creek.

Palmetto Braid, Hats, Etc.

The art of working the Palmetto into the different articles of usefulness was probably obtained from the Florida Indians; and since then has been put to a good use by the inhabitants of St. Augustine, though the articles, at that time manufactured, were confined entirely to home or individual use.

Since 1868, Palmetto has been extensively worked into the different styles and patterns of braid for ladies', gentlemens' and childrens' hats; including numerous fancy articles which meet with ready sale among the visitors.

Of late the manufacturers of Palmetto braid, in St. Augustine, have received large orders from houses in the several leading cities at the North, for the different patterns of braid. Frequent shipments have been made to Paris, there to be made into hats of the latest foreign fashions.

At one time there was quite a demand at the North for this style of goods ; and many were induced to embark in the business, in which their expectations of gain were not realized.

It is estimated that the amount of goods disposed of at that time amounted to $60,000. Ladies' and Gentlemens' hats are to be found for sale by the several *artistes* in this vocation. These goods are well made, tastefully trimmed, and command a ready sale to visitors.

The manufacture of Lace, by the Sisters of the Convent, will, it is said, equal in quality, design and finish, that made in foreign countries. The making of lace is also indulged in by the young ladies of St. Augustine.

The Post Office.

The Post Office is located in the once Spanish Governor's Palace, occupying the front ground floor and overlooking the Plaza. During the Winter season, the Northern mail arrives every afternoon; the departures occur each forenoon.

The Thermometer.

The equal temperature is one of the excellences of the climate of Florida. The Thermometer very rarely falls below 30 degrees, or rises above 95 degrees. According to the old Spanish record, kept at St. Augustine, for one hundred years, the temperature averaged a little over 60 degrees.

Orange Groves and Gardens.

St. Augustine and its environs possesses many fine orange groves and elegant gardens; and a pleasing sight it is to the stranger and tourist to witness these attractions in the Ancient City; to admire the green orange groves with the ripe, delicious fruit hanging in golden clusters from the over loaded branches; to inhale the delightful odor of the sweet orange blossoms, and to look upon the green and the ripe fruit both claiming the same tree, a coincidence rarely to be met with on this continent.

In the gardens of St. Augustine we also find the banana, fig, Japan plum, pomegranate and other rare semi-tropical fruits; and one may also observe many varieties of plants and flowers beautifully arranged about the many handsome residences located in and about the city.

Hotels, and Boarding Houses.

The St. Augustine Hotel, E. E. Vaill & Co., Proprietors. Fronting on the Plaza. Accommodation for about two hundred guests. $ 4. per day.

The Magnolia Hotel, W. W. Palmer, Proprietor. Located on St George street, north of the Plaza. Accommodates one hundred and twenty-five guests. $ 4. per day.

The Florida House, J. H. Remer, Proprietor. Located on St. George and Treasury Streets. Accommodation for about two hundred guests. $ 4. per day.

The Oriental Hotel, W. G. Ponce & Co., Proprietors. On the American and European plan. Located on Charlotte street. Accommodates sixty guests. $ 3. per day.

BOARDING HOUSES.

Mrs. M. L. Abbott, located on Marine street, south of the Plaza. Accommodation for about 30 guests. Board from $ 12. to $ 15. per week.

Miss Julia Stinson, located on St. George street, north of the Magnolia hotel; accommodations for about 20 guests. $ 12. to $ 15. per week.

Mrs. J. V. Hernandez, located on Charlotte street, north of the Plaza. Accommodates about 40 guests, $ 10. to $ 15. per week.

Mrs. Couper Gibbs, located on Marine street, south of the Plaza. Accommodates about 30 guests. $ 15. per week.

E. J. Medicis, situated on the south end of St. George street. Accommodates about 25 guests. $ 10. to $ 12. per week.

Mrs. C. H. Paterson, located on Bay street, can accommodate about 25 guests; $ 15. per week.

Also Mrs. Geo. S. Greeno, located on Marine street; and Miss Fatio, located on Hospital street; both places are situated south of the Plaza.

There are a number of private houses that extend accommodation to the invalid and tourist.

Miscellaneous.

Troy is 148 miles, Boston, 230, Philadelphia, Pa., 88, Washington, D. C., 230, Richmond, Va.·, 358, Charleston, S. Ca., 817, Macon, Ga., 1055, Atlanta, Ga., 952, Chattanooga, Tenn., 850, Savannah, Ga., 877, (by water, 716 miles), Jacksonville, Fla., 1130, St. Augustine, Fla, 1193, Palatka, Fla., 1205, and Enterprise, Fla., 1341.

When it is noon at Washington it is at Atlanta, Ga, 11,30 a. m., Charleston, S. C., 11,43 a. m., Key West, Fla., 11,41 a. m., New Orleans, La., 11,08 a. m., New York, 12,12 p. m., Norfolk, Va., 12,03 p. m., Richmond, Va., 11,58 a. m., Savannah, Ga., 11,44 a. m., St. Augustine, Fla., 11,42 a. m., and Jacksonville, Fla., 11,42 a. m.

Tourists who expect to see the State of Florida thoroughly should not fail to procure a good map of the same. A very neat and complete pocket map is published by Columbus Drew, Bookseller, at Jacksonville.

A good pair of Field or Opera Glasses will be found very convenient. There are many objects which they could be brought to bear upon with interest.

Florida is the best timbered State in the Union. It has over 30,000,000 acres.

The census of Florida, in 1870, gives a total population of 187,000 ; 96,000 white, and 91,000 colored.

Tallahassee, the capital, has a population of about 3000. Fernandina about 3000. Jacksonville about 14,000. St. Augustine 2000. Lake City 1200. Pensacola 2500. Gainesville 1800. Quincy 900. Key West about 5500. Palatka 1500.

The Atlantic and Gulf Railroad, from Savannah to Jacksonville, was re-laid with steel rails during the summer of 1874. The road, with its first-class paraphernalia, presents to the traveler safety, comfort and quick time.

We would call attention to the excellent workmanship displayed upon the Title page of this Guide, which was executed by Messrs. Winham & Arnold, of 103 Fulton Street, New York.

This Guide will be re-issued on or about the 1st of November, 1875; and we would call the attention of all Railroad Managers and Hotel Proprietors, interested in the matter of Florida travel—should they desire to take advantage of our circulation—to send us any such information as may be of use to tourists and others, before the 30th of October next. We request that such information, regarding routes—rail and water—and hotels, may be correct for the months of Dec., Jan., Feb., Mar., Apr. and to the 15th of May ensuing. We shall spare no pains to gather all and every such information as may be of value to the tourist, traveler or invalid. Address J. P. Whitney, P. O. Box 522, N. Y. City.

To Advertisers.

Our rates for advertising in the "FLORIDA PATHFINDER" will be as follows :

One page - - - - -	$30.00
Half " - - - - -	15.00
Quarter " - - - - -	8.00

HOTELS ON THE ROUTE.

RICHMOND, Va.

The Exchange Hotel and Ballard House, J. L. Carington, Proprietor. $3. per day.

The St. James Hotel, F. W. Hoeninger, assisted by John P. Ballard. $3. per day.

Ford's Hotel, A. J. Ford, Proprietor. $2.50 per day.

The American Hotel, N. Cobb, Prop. $2.50 per day.

The St Charles Hotel, — Moore, Propr. $2. per day.

NORFOLK, Va.

The Atlantic Hotel, R. S. Dobson, Propr. $3. per day.

The National Hotel, Holt & Bro., Props., $2.50 per day.

PETERSBURG, Va.

The Jarratt House. $3 per day.

WILMINGTON, N. C.

The Purcell House, J. R. Davis, Prop., $4 per day.

The National Hotel. $3 per day.

FLORENCE, N. C.

The Gamble House.

COLUMBIA, S. C.

The Wheeler House,

The Columbia House, Gorham & Calnan, Props.,

AUGUSTA, Ga.

Planters' Hotel, B. P. Chatfield, Prop., B. F. Brown, Manager.

AIKEN, S. C.

Highland Park Hotel, B. P. Chatfield, Prop., E. H. Tomlinson, Manager.

ATLANTA, Ga.

The Kimball House. G. McGinly, Prop., $3 to $4 p. day.

MACON, Ga.

Brown's Hotel.

The Spotswood House.

The Lanier House.

The Planters' Hotel.

CHARLESTON.

The Charleston Hotel, E. H. Jackson & Co., Proprietors. $4. per day.

The Pavillion Hotel, G. T. Alford & Co., Props., $3 p. day.

The Waverly House. $3 per day.

The Mills House. $2.50 per day.

SAVANNAH.

The Pulaski House, S. N. Papot & Co., Prop's. $4. per day.

The Screven House, R. Bradley, Propr. $4. per day.

The Marshall House, A. B. Luce, Propr. $3. per day.

Bresnan's European House, John Bresnan. Proprietor, Board and room $2.00 per day.

FERNANDINA, Fla.

The Riddell House, Samuel T. Riddell, Prop. $2.50 per day.

The Norwood House, J. S. Mooney, Propr. $2. per day.

JACKSONVILLE, FLORIDA.

The Grand National Hotel, George McGinly, Proprietor. $4. per day.

The St. James Hotel, Campbell & Andrews, Proprietors, $4. per day.

The Metropolitan Hotel, J.B. Togni, Propr. $3 per day. Also, The Florida Home, J. J. Comfort. The St. John's House, Mrs. E. Hudnall. There are numerous boarding houses among which we mention those of the Misses Mattair, Buffington, Keen, Stickney, etc.

Hotels on the St. John's River.

HIBERNIA. Mrs. Fleming, keeps a commodious establishment. $3. per day.

MAGNOLIA. The Magnolia Hotel, E. R. Houghton, Proprietor. $4. per day.

GREEN COVE SPRING. The Clarendon Hotel, Harris & Applegate, Proprietors. $4. per day.

The Union Hotel, Charles Houghton, Mangr. $4. per day.

TOCOI. There is a Restaurant kept by J. C. Thomas for the accommodation of travelers to St. Augustine.

PALATKA. The St. John's Hotel, P. & H. Peterman, Proprietors. $3.50 per day.

The Putnam House, H. L. Hart, Prop. $3.50 per day.

SAN MATTEO. The Riversdale House, J. M. H. Miller, Proprietor. $2.50 per day.

MELLONVILLE. The Mellonville House, I. I. Hite, Prop. $3. per day. Also boarding house accommodations.

ENTERPRISE. The Brock House, Mr. —— Carr, Propr. Board $3. per day.

Ticket Agencies.

BOSTON.—Nos. 77, 82, 86 and 87 Washington Street, and 3 Old State House.

NEW YORK CITY.—Nos. 1 and 9 Astor House. Nos. 315, 397, 526, 944 Broadway, and all Pennsylvania Railroad Ticket Offices.

PHILADELPHIA.—Nos. 700, 732, 838, under the Continental Hotel, Chestnut Street, corner of Broad and Chestnut Sts., and at P. W. & D. D. Depot.

31

Piedmont Air Line R. R.

C. YINGLING, AGENT, 9 ASTOR HOUSE, BROADWAY.

Leave New York via "Pennyslvania Railroad"—Jersey City at 9 p.m. take Pullman's sleeping cars to Washington* arriving at Philadelphia 12.35 a.m. thence to Baltimore, via "Philadelphia, Wilmington & Baltimore Railroad," arrive 4.20 a. m. thence to Washington via "Baltimore & Potomac Railroad," arrive 5.45 a. m., leave Washington at 7 a.m, thence to Quantico via steamer on the Potomac river —meals $1 extra. Arrive at Quantico 9.30 a.m.; thence to Richmond, via "Richmond, Fredericksburg & Potomac Railroad," arrive at Richmond* 1.30 p.m.—dinner; here take Pullman's sleeping car to Charlotte. Leave Richmond 2:05 p. m. at Fredericksburg & Potomac Junction, via "Richmond & Danville Railroad," arrive at Clover Station 6.46 p.m—supper. Arrive at Charlotte* 6.22 a.m.—breakfast—leave Charlotte via "Charlotte, Columbia & Augusta Railroad" 7.30 a. m. arrive at Columbia 2.13 p. m.—dinner Arrive at Granitville 6.40 p. m.—partake of supper. At this point connection is made with the "So. Carolina Railroad" for Aiken; (five miles distant.) Leave Granitville 7.15 p. m. and arrive at Augusta 8.00 p. m. leave 8.05 p.m. —take sleeping car—via "Central Railroad of Georgia," arriving at Savannah 7.15 a. m.–breakfast. Omnibus transfer. "See Savannah connections."

Piedmont Air Line.

VIA CHARLOTTE, ATLANTA TO JACKSONVILLE.

See previous route from N. Y. to Charlotte*. Leave Charlotte 6.22 a. m.; partake of breakfast, arrive at Central station 1.48 p.m.—dinner ; arrive at Norcross 7.54 p.m. – supper ; arrive at Atlanta* 9.18 p.m. (48 hours from New York), thence via "Macon & Brunswick Railroad" ; leave Atlanta 9.40 p.m. ; arrive at Macon 7.10 a.m. arrive at Jesup* 6.45 p.m., on the "Atlantic & Gulf Railroad"— partake of supper ; arrive at Jacksonville, Fla. 10.12 a.m. see "Up the St. John's River."

Piedmont Air Line.

VIA YORK RIVER ROUTE.

Leave New York 8.40 a.m.; leave Philadelphia at 12.15 p.m.; arrive at Baltimore* 3.50 p.m., here take one of the splendid Bay steamers of the York River Line on the Chesapeake Bay, at 4.00 p. m.; get supper, stateroom and breakfast on steamer; arrive at West Point at 8.00 a.m.; thence via Richmond & York River R. R. to Richmond*; arriving at 10.00 a.m.; take dinner and leave Richmond at 1.38 p.m., via Richmond & Danville R. R. Route, same from Richmond as Piedmont Air Line above to all points south.

Piedmont Air Line.

VIA OLD DOMINION STEAMSHIP LINE.

Leave New York, via Old Dominion Steamship to Richmond; leave pier 37 North river every Tuesday, Thursday and Saturday at 3 p.m.; arriving at Richmond second day at noon; thence Piedmont Air Line, via Richmond & Danville R. R. Division, leaving at 1.38 p.m.; thence, as previous schedules, via Piedmont Air Line to all points south.

Atlantic Coast Line R. R.

ALL RAIL—VIA WILMINGTON, COLUMBIA, AUGUSTA TO SAVANNAH.

Leave New York—or Jersey City via "Pennsylvania Railroad"—take Pullman's Parlor car leaving at 3 p. m., without change to Washington,* arriving at 10.30 p. m. Leave Washington 11.33 p. m., via "Richmond, Fredericksburg & Potomac Railroad" arriving at Richmond 4.50 a. m., leave Richmond 5.05 a.m., arrive at Petersburg 6.15 a. m.—breakfast here; leave at 6.22 a. m., arrive at Weldon* 9.25 a. m., leave Weldon 9.50 a. m., via "Wilmington & Weldon Railroad," arrive at Goldsboro 1.52 p. m. —partake of dinner. Arrive at Wilmington* 5.50 p. m.— here partake of supper. Leave Wilmington via "Wilmington, Columbia and Augusta Railroad," at 6.10 p.m.—take Pullman's sleeping car to Augusta, arrive at Florence 11.-37 p.m. arrive at Columbia 4 a.m., arrive at Granitville and partake of breakfast at 7.40 a. m., arrive at Augusta* 8.40 a.m., take Pullman's sleeping car, leave 8.45 a.m., via "Central Railroad of Georgia," arrive at Savannah 7.15 a.m. Omnibus transfer—see hotels on the route—see "Savannah connections."

Atlantic Coast Line.

VIA CHARLESTON TO SAVANNAH.

From New York to Wilmington* as in the previous route. Leave Wilmington 6.10 p. m. via "Wilmington, Columbia & Augusta" Road. Take Pullman's sleeping car— arrive at Florence at 11.37 thence via "North-eastern Railroad" to Charleston,* arriving 5.35 a. m.—breakfast; omnibus transfer to " Savannah & Charleston Railroad," leave Charleston 8.00 a. m. Arrive at Savannah* 3.0J p. m. See "Savannah connections." For additional information regarding the "Atlantic Coast" Line, etc., apply at 397 Broadway, New York.

The Bay Route.

"ATLANTIC COAST LINE."

VIA RAIL TO BALTIMORE, STEAMER TO PORTSMOUTH, RAIL TO WELDON, WILLMINGTON, COLUMBIA, AUGUSTA AND SAVANNAH.

Leave New York via "Pennsylvania Railroad"—Jersey City, leave at 8.40 a.m. for Baltimore ; arrive at Philadelphia ; leave via "Philadelphia, Wilmington & Baltimore Railroad," at 12.15 noon, arrive at Baltimore 3.55 p.m. Omnibus transfer to the "Bay Line" of steamers; meals and state-rooms each $1 extra. Leave Baltimore 4 p.m., arrive at Portsmouth at 5.50 a.m., leave 6.00 a.m. via "Seaboard & Roanoke Railroad;" arrive at Weldon* 9.25 a.m.; thence, same as in Atlantic Coast Line, first schedule.

Virginia Midland Route.

Leave New York.—Jersey City via Pennsylvania Railroad at 9.00 p.m., take Sleeping Car to Baltimore or Washington. Arrive at Philadelphia 12.40 a.m. Arrive at Baltimore 4.40 a.m.; thence to Washington, arrive 6.20 a.m.; thence via the Virginia Midland Route, arrive at Alexandria 7.40 a.m—breakfast. Arrive at Lynchburg 5 p.m.; Danville* at 8.50 p.m. Arrive at Charlotte* 6.30 a.m.—breakfast; thence either by way of Augusta and Savannah, or via Columbia and Charleston, or via Atlanta, Macon and Jesup to Jacksonville. For tickets, schedules and additional information, apply at the office of the "Virginia Midland Railroad," G. M. Huntington, Agent, 315 Broadway.

The Old Dominion S. S. Line.

VIA WILMINGTON & CHARLESTON TO SAVANNAH.

OFFICE 197 GREENWICH ST., COR. FULTON.

Sailing from Pier 37 North River, at 3 p. m. The side-wheel steamship "Wyanoke," Capt. Couch, leaves every Tuesday. The side-wheel steamer "Isaac Bell," Capt. Blakeman, leaves every Thursday. The side-wheel steamer "Old Dominion," Capt. Valker, leaves every Saturday. Arrive on the following day at Portsmouth, 5 p.m. leave Portsmouth 6 o'clock following morning via "Seaboard & Roanoke Railroad," arrive at Weldon 9.30 a.m. leave Weldon at 9.50 a. m. via " Wilmington & Weldon Railroad," .arrive at Wilmington* 5.50 p. m. leave at 6.10 p. m. via " Wilmington, Columbia & Augusta Railroad," arrive at Florence at 11.27 p. m. leave at 11.30 p. m. via "Northeastern Railroad" for Charleston, arriving at 5.35 a. m. Omnibus transfer, breakfast at hotel. Leave Charleston via "Savannah & Charleston Railroad" 8.00 a. m. arrive at Savannah* 3.00 p. m. See "Savannah Connections."

The Old Dominion S. S. Line.

VIA WILMINGTON, COLUMBIA & AUGUSTA TO SAVANNAH.

Arrive at Florence 11.27 p.m. as in the foregoing route; arrive at Columbia 4 a.m., arrive at Granitville and partake of breakfast at 7.40 a.m. arrive at Augusta* 8.40 a.m., leave 8.45 a.m., via "Central Railroad of Georgia," arrive at Savannah 5.25 p. m. Omnibus transfer—see hotels on the route—see "Savannah connections."

N. Y. & Charleston S. S. Co.

JAMES W. QUINTARD & CO., AGENTS, 177 WEST ST. N. Y.

Comprising the following elegant side-wheel steamships : The "Manhattan," Capt. M. S. Woodhull. The "Champion," Capt. R. W. Lockwood. The "James Adger," Capt. T. J. Lockwood. The "Georgia," Capt. S. Crowell. The "South Carolina," Capt. J. T. Beckett. The "Charleston," Capt. James Berry.

One of the above steamers leaves Pier 29 North River, foot of Warren street, every Tuesday, Thursday and Saturday at 3 o'clock p. m.

By leaving New York on the Tuesday steamer the traveler arrives at Charleston on Friday morning. Thursday's steamer arrives at Charleston Sunday morning. Saturday's steamer arrives at Charleston on Tuesday morning.

Excursion tickets are issued by this route at greatly reduced rates to all interesting points in connection with a trip to Florida These tickets are sold over the following route. New. York to Charleston by the above steamers, thence by the steamers "Dictator" and " City Point," to Savannah, Fernandina, Jacksonville and all landings on the St. John's river.. Prices of Excursion tickets as follows. Fernandina $50; Jacksonville $50; Green Cove Spring $54; St Augustine $58; Palatka $54. Tickets good until July 1875. " See Charleston connections."

Charleston Connections.

The steamer Dictator, Captain Vogel, leaves every Friday evening at 8 o'clock. Arrives at Savannah; leaves Savannah Wednesday noon, arriving the same evening at . Fernandina; arrives next morning at Jacksonville, and at all points on the St. John's River; arriving at Palatka at 4 p.m.

The steamer City Point, Captain Fitzgerald, leaves Charleston every Saturday evening at 8 o'clock. Arrives at Savannah; leaves Savannah at noon on Sunday; arrives same evening at Fernandina; arrives next morning at Jacksonville and all points on the St. John's River; arriving at Palatka at 4 p.m.

"SAVANNAH & CHARLESTON RAILROAD."—Leave Charleston 8.00 a.m., arrive at Savannah following afternoon 3.00 p.m. Leave Charleston 5 p.m. arrive at Savannah 11.45 p.m.

Savannah Steamships.
"MURRAY LINE."

Murray, Ferris & Co., Agents, 62 South Street, New York. The steamship "Leo," Capt. G. A. Dearborn. The steamship "Cleopatra," Captain E. M. Bulkley. Steamer sailing every Tuesday from Pier 16, East River; at 3 o'clock p.m., arriving at Savannah Friday morning.

Savannah Steamships
"THE EMPIRE LINE."

Wm. R. Garrison, Agent, 5 Bowling Green, New York. The Steamships "Herman Livingstone," Captain J. H. Mallory, and "Gen. Barnes," Captain G. H. Cheeseman, sail alternately from Pier 43 North River, every Thursday, at 3 p.m. arrive at Savannah on Sunday morning.

The steamships "San Salvador," Captain G. Nickerson, and "San Jacinto," Captain F. Hazard, sail alternately from Pier 43 North River every Saturday at 3 p.m., arriving at Savannah on Tuesday morning.

Savannah Steamships.
"THE BLACK STAR LINE."

R. Lowden, agent, 93 West Street. The steamships "Montgomery," Captain C. R. Faircloth, and "Huntsville," Captain W. L. Crowell, sail alternately from Pier 12 North River, every Saturday at 3 p.m., arrive at Savannah on Tuesday morning.

Miscellaneous Information.

Fare by the Savannah Steamships to Savannah $20 ; to Fernandina and Jacksonville $27.75; Hibernia and Green Cove Spring $28.75; St. Augustine $31.75; Palatka $29.-75, Enterprise $35.75. See "Savannah connections."

Excursion tickets are issued by the Savannah Steamships at greatly reduced rates to all interesting points in connection with a trip to Florida. These tickets are sold over the following route. New York to Savannah by the above steamers, thence by the steamers "Dictator" and "City Point," to Fernandina, Jacksonville and all landings on the St. John's river. Prices of excursion tickets as follows, Fernandina, $50; Green Cove Spring $54; St. Augustine $58; Palatka $54. Tickets good until July 1875. These tickets are good by the steamer "Lizzie Baker" (inside route) to Florida; and will probably be accepted by the "Atlantic & Gulf" Railroad from Savannah to Jacksonville, thence via the St. John's River steamers, etc. "See Savannah connections."

Parties intending leaving New York by the Savannah Steamships, and desirous of making connection with the steamer "Lizzie Baker" for points in Florida, should leave New York on the Saturday's Steamer, arriving at Savannah on Tuesday evening, thence by the (Inland Route) steamer "Lizzie Baker," leaving Wednesday at 9 a.m.

Savannah Connections.

THE ATLANTIC & GULF R. R. TO JACKSONVILLE.

Leave Savannah 4.00 p.m. daily—take Pullman's sleeping car through to Jacksonville without change; arrive at Jesup 7.35 p.m. partake of supper; at this point connection is made with the "Macon & Brunswick" Railroad, with train from Atlanta, etc. Leave Jesup 7.55 p.m. and arrive at Du Pont 12.30 a. m. Arrive at Live Oak 3.35 a.m; arrive at Baldwin 8.07 a. m.—breakfast, here connect with railroad for Cedar Keys, arrive at Jacksonville 10,00 a. m. It is intended that this train will make close connection with the St. John's River Steamer "Florence" for all points on the river, etc. The above train leaves Savannah daily.

Leave Savannah 8.30 a.m., arrive at Tebeauville 1.12 p.m.—dinner. Arrive at Lake City 6.39 p.m.—supper. Arrive at Jacksonville 10.20 p.m. This train leaves Savannah daily (Sundays excepted) during the height of the Florida travel.

Savannah Connections.

STEAMER "LIZZIE BAKER," INLAND ROUTE.

The steamer "Lizzie Baker," Captain P. La Rose, leaves Savannah—Padelford's Wharf every Wednesday at 9 A.M. for Doboy, Brunswick; arriving at St. Mary's on Thursday morning, touching at Fernandina the same morning, and arriving at Jacksonville at 12 noon; stopping at all points on the St. John's River. Arriving at Tocoi 3.30 P. M; arrive at Palatka Thursday evening.

Returning, leave Palatka on the following morning, connecting at Tocoi with the train from St. Augustine, touching at all points on the St. John's River. Arrive at Jacksonville. Leave 3 A. M. (or to suit the tide) Friday, arriving at Savannah Sunday noon.

Up the St. John's River.

BROCK'S LINE OF STEAMERS.

The steamer "Florence" leaves Jacksonville daily (Sundays excepted,) at 9 a.m. or on the arrival of the train on the "Atlantic and Gulf Railroad" from Savannah, for all points on the St. John's river, terminating at Palatka. The steamer arrives at Manderin 10.30 a. m; Hibernia 11.30 a. m ; Magnolia 12 noon ; Green Cove Spring 12.30 p. m; Picolata 1.30 p. m; Tocoi 1.50 p. m; Connect here with the St. John's Railroad for St. Augustine. During the Summer of 1874, the road was relaid with modern T • rails, and trains complete the trip, a distance of 14 miles in about 40 minutes; Arrive at Palatka 3.30 p. m.; connection is here made with the St. John's River steamer "Hattie," which leaves Palatka every Monday, Wednesday and Friday for Enterprise. Steamers leave Jacksonville and Palatka for the Oclawaha River, the Lakes Harney, Jessup, Harris, Eustis and Griffin, the several Springs, and other points of interest.

Local Fare on the St. John's River: from Jacksonville and intermediate landings to Green Cove Spring, $1.00; all points beyond Green Cove Spring to ·Palatka, $2.00. Meals $1.00 extra. Jacksonville to Mellonville and Enterprise, including meals and stateroom, $9.00. Palatka to Mellonville and Enterprise, including meals and stateroom, $6.00. The time occupied in a trip from Jacksonvilla to Enterprise is about thirty-five hours. Fare from Savannah (by Rail) to Jacksonville, $7.00. Fare from Jacksonville to St. Augustine, $4.00.

A FAVORITE ROUTE TO

FLORIDA

—Is Via—

THE OLD DOMINION STEAMSHIP LINE,

Comprising the elegant Side-Wheel
Passenger Steamers

" *Old Dominion,*"
" *Wyanoke,*" and
" *Isaac Bell,*"

SAILING EVERY

Tuesday, Thursday and Saturday,

FROM PIER **37** NORTH RIVER AT **3** O'CLOCK, P.M.

FOR NORFOLK,

thence by ATLANTIC COAST LINE RAILWAYS, via
Wilmington, Charleston and Savannah, or via Wilmington, Columbia, Augusta to

SAVANNAH;

thence via Rail or Water to

FLORIDA.

For Through Tickets and additional information, apply
at the office of THE OLD DOMINION STEAMSHIP Co.,

197 GREENWICH ST. (Cor. Fulton) NEW YORK.

Returning, leave Norfolk every Monday, Wednesday and
Saturday, at 7.30 P. M. (except for a short time in the
middle of winter when steamers will leave at 4 P. M.) on
arrival of Southern trains.

Tickets by this route include Meals and Stateroom.
Baggage checked to destination. For additional information, apply at office of

OLD DOMINION S. S. CO.,

197 Greenwich St., New York.

Great Southern Freight and Passenger Route Via
SAVANNAH, GA.

For Florida and all Points in the South and South-West.

One of the following First-Class Steamships will sail as
follows, punctually at 3 P. M.

MURRAY LINE, from Pier 16, East River, foot of Wall Street,

LEO. CLEOPATRA.

Murray, Ferris & Co., Agents, 62 South Street.

EMPIRE LINE, Every Thursday, from Pier 43, North River.

Herman Livingston, Gen. Barnes,

Every Saturday, from Pier 43, North River.

San Salvador, San Jacinto,

Wm. R. Garrison, Agent, 5 Bowling Green.

BLACK STAR LINE, Every Saturday, from Pier 12, North River,

Huntsville, Montgomery,

R. Lowden, Agent, 93 West St.

Making close connection at Savannah with the CENTRAL Railroad
of Georgia, for all points in the South and South-West. And with the
Atlantic and Gulf Railroad for all points in Florida.

FOR ST. JOHN'S RIVER & ST. AUGUSTINE,

Passengers have choice of Three Routes from Savannah:

1st. ATLANTIC & GULF RAILROAD. Trains leave
SAVANNAH Morning and Evening. Night Express going through to
JACKSONVILLE, without change, making close connections with
ST. JOHN'S RIVER STEAMBOATS.

Pullman's Palace Sleeping Cars on all Night Trains.

2d. Steamer **"LIZZIE BAKER,"** from SAVANNAH, by
Inside Route through the Sounds.

3d. Steamers "CITY POINT" and "DICTATOR,"
of Outside Line from SAVANNAH.

N. B.—Passengers for ST. AUGUSTINE land at Tocoi, thence by ST.
JOHN'S R. R.

Railroad Tickets good by either Line of Steamers.

On comparison, this will be found to be the Cheapest as well as the
Most Delightful Route to the above Points.

The rates to many points, are Forty to Fifty per cent. less than the
ALL RAIL ROUTE, the TIME made being NEARLY AS SHORT,
with the addition of a Table furnished with the Luxuries of the season
without additional expense.

Trains leave SAVANNAH Morning and Evening. SLEEPING
CARS on all night Trains.

THROUGH RATES OF FREIGHT GIVEN AND THROUGH BILLS
OF LADING SIGNED TO ALL POINTS.

For further particulars, freight or passage, apply to

MURRAY, FERRIS & CO., 62 South Street,
WM. R. GARRISON, 2 Bowling Green,
R. LOWDEN, 93 West Street.

Chas. W. Harwood, Agent, George Yonge, Agent,
Atlantic & Gulf R. R. 315 Broadway. Central R. R. of Georgia, 409 Broadway.

FOR FLORIDA,

THE

First-Class New-York Built Steamers

DICTATOR, - Capt. Vogel,
CITY POINT, Capt. Fitzgerald.

Connect at CHARLESTON and SAVANNAH with the
New York Steamers and Northern Trains for

SAVANNAH, FERNANDINA, JACK-SONVILLE, ST. AUGUSTINE, HIBERNIA, MAGNOLIA, GREEN COVE Springs, PALATKA.

Including all Landings on the St. John's River,

CONNECT AT PALATKA WITH STEAMERS FOR ENTERPRISE,
MELLONVILLE. SANFORD AND INDIAN RIVER, ALSO
WITH STEAMERS FOR THE OCKLAWAHA RIVER.

All Through Railroad Tickets to

FLORIDA

Received on these Steamers in Payment of Passage.

No Extra Charge for Meals or Stateroom.

VISITORS TO FLORIDA,

Whether pleasure-seekers or invalids, will find the route by the DIC-TATOR and CITY POINT the most enjoyable and the least expensive; it is the only route by which the beautiful scenery of the lower St. John's River can be viewed, with the many points rendered interesting, as the scences of the earliest settlements on the Continent, and of the many bloody struggles between the French and Spaniards.

Those traveling with invalids—ladies or children, will particularly appreciate the trouble and anxiety avoided, by being carried direct to their destination without several times having to shift baggage, etc., etc.

The steamers are of the safest description, especially adapted to the service—fitted with every comfort and convenience—clean, comfortable Staterooms, a table provided with every luxury of the Charleston, Savannah and Florida markets, and equal to that of any first-class hotel.

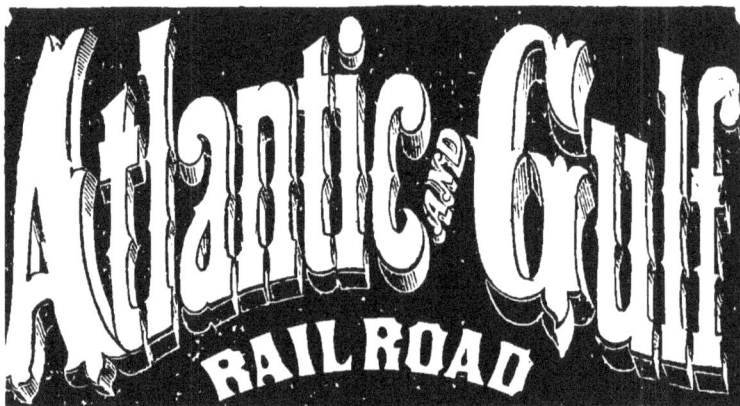

For Florida.

Inland Route !   No Sea sickness !
Fast Time !   Superior Accommodations !

THE ELEGANT PASSENGER STEAMER

LIZZIE BAKER,

LA ROSE, Commander.

WILL LEAVE

Savannah every Wednesday 9 a.m.

FOR

*FERNANDINA, JACKSONVILLE,
PALATKA and Intermediate Landings on the ST. JOHN'S RIVER.*

Connecting at Tocoi with St. John's R.R. for St. Augustine; at Palatka with steamers for Mellonville, Enterprise
and all points on the Upper St. John's and Oclawaha
Rivers. Arriving at Jacksonville Thursday Morning, Palatka Thursday Night.

RETURNING,

Will leave Palatka Friday Morning; Jacksonville Saturday
Morning. Arriving at Savannah Sunday.

A. L. RICHARDSON, Gen'l Agent,
SAVANNAH, Ga,

St. Augustine Hotel

St. Augustine, Fla.,

E. E. VAILL & CO.,

Proprietors.

This spacious and elegant hotel is now open to the public; having been entirely re-furnished,   It has a Southerly front, of 200 feet, on the Plaza, with wide piazzas from each story overlooking "Ye Ancient City," the Bay, Rivers and the Atlantic Ocean.

The St. Augustine Hotel is first-class in every particular, being lighted with gas, and having the additions of an Ice house—whence ice can be obtained at all times—a hot and cold salt-water bath-house, a billiard room, bowling alley, etc.

The completion of the R.R. from Tocoi places the traveller within 45 minutes of the St. John's River and relieves him from all delay.

THE

Magnolia Hotel,

St. George Street,

St. Augustine,   Florida.

W. W. Palmer, Proprietor.

THE

Florida House,

ST. AUGUSTINE, FLA.

J. H. REMER, Proprietor.

The Proprietor of the above Hotel has just completed an Extension to his Hotel, 125x25 feet, four stories high, with every modern improvement. The rooms are spacious, airy and furnished with every comfort and convenience. The whole establishment is carpeted with elegant Brussels carpeting, and furnished with an abundance of handsome Black-Walnut furniture.

IT IS IN EVERY RESPECT A

First - Class Hotel.

The chambers are larger, more sunny and better arranged than those of other establishments in the city.

Parties visiting the city are invited to call and inspect for themselves.

G. K. MITCHELL,

ARCHITECT AND BUILDER,

St. George Street,   St. Augustine.
Refers to Hon. John F. Whitney,   Isaac Stone, Esq.,
Geo. Burt, Esq.,   Thomas Pacetti, Esq.

DR. J. HUME SIMONS,

Practitioner of

Medicine and Surgery,

St. Augustine,   Fla..

W. Howell Robinson,

ATTORNEY & COUNSELLOR AT LAW,

Office at Residence, on Hospital Street.

MRS. ABBOTT'S

FIRST CLASS

Private Boarding House,

Marine Street, South of the Plaza.

TERMS— $12. to $15. per week.

ESTABLISHED 1867.

Lights and Fires included.   Open the entire year.

Miss Julia Stinson,

FIRST-CLASS

PRIVATE BOARDING HOUSE,

ST. GEORGE STREET,

North of the Magnolia Hotel.

TERMS $12 TO $15 PER WEEK.

MRS. J. V. HERNANDEZ,

STILL CONTINUES HER

First-Class Boarding House

On CHARLOTTE STREET, opposite the well-known Aurora House, kept by her for the past 5 years, and in which she gave perfect satisfaction. She has now accommodations for about 40 guests. Terms from $10 to $15 per week, or transient $2 per day.

MRS. B. F. OLIVEROS,

MANUFACTURER OF

Fancy Palmetto Work and Hats.

ST. GEORGE STREET,

North of the Magnolia Hotel.

MRS. MARY HERNANDEZ,

Manufacturer of Ladies & Gentlemens'

FLORIDA PALMETTO HATS,

FINE WORK A SPECIALTY.

North of the Plaza, West of St. George Street and South of the City Gate,

ST. AUGUSTINE, Florida.

Grand National Hotel,

JACKSONVILLE, Fla.

GEO. McGINLY, - - *Proprietor.*

$4.00 Per Day.

This elegant and commodious Brick House, of modern structure and furnished with elegant furniture, is situated within two hundred yards of the Railroad Depot, and is unsurpassed by any Hotel in the South.

H. I. Kimball House

ATLANTA, GA.

The attention of Winter Tourists to the South is respectfully called to the fact that the undersigned, having leased the above house, has had it thoroughly renovated and refitted during the past season, and is now prepared to accommodate, comfortably, 550 guests.

The rooms are furnished in the most luxurious style, and the *cuisine* is presided over by an experienced head-steward, with a corps of French cooks, unequaled in their line.

The Billiard Room has been frescoed, and supplied with eight new Phelan & Collender tables.

N. B.—Guests will find this THE hotel to stop at in Atlanta.

Rooms secured by telegraph in advance to

GEO. McGINLY, Proprietor.

Wholesale and Retail Dealer in

Choice Family Groceries,

Provisions, Confectionery

AND FRUITS.

Also, JOHN T. WILSON & CO'S

CHOICE CRACKERS & BISCUITS.

Ales, Wines, Liquors,

SEGARS AND TOBACCO.

NEW STORE:

Bay Street, bet. Pine and Laura Streets,

JACKSONVILLE, FLA.

DREW'S MAP OF FLORIDA,

For the Pocket.   Price, - - - - - $1.25
FAIRBANK'S HISTORY OF FLORIDA,
Price, $2.50.   Postage, 25 cents.
FAIRBANK'S HISTORY OF ST. AUGUSTINE,
Price, $1.   Mailed upon receipt of price.   Address

COLUMBUS DREW,

BOOKSELLER AND STATIONER,
JACKSONVILLE, FLORIDA.

J. H. CROWELL,

DEALER IN

Boots, Shoes, Leather & Findings.

CASH PAID FOR

HIDES, SKINS, FURS, WAX, WOOL, &C.

JACKSONVILLE, Fla.

AND

Exchange Hotel,

RICHMOND, VA.

J. L. CARRINGTON, - - *Proprietor.*

These leading Fashionable Hotels have been newly and elegantly furnished, and are now ready to extend a Virginia welcome to their Patrons.

THE

Pavilion Hotel

Cor. Bull & South Broad Sts.,

SAVANNAH, GA.

A FAMILY HOTEL

Of Old Standing,

Possessing all the advantages and requirements of a quiet and genial home.

P. J. HOBART, Proprietor.

Johnson Square,

SAVANNAH, GA.,

Facing South, with a Frontage of 273 Feet.

S. N. PAPOT & CO., Proprietors.

This well-known Hotel, which has always been considered the leading Hotel in Savannah, and one of the best in the South, is pleasantly located in the central portion of the city, on Johnson Square, with a southern front, which is a matter of no small importance in this climate. In consequence of the death of the late proprietor, Major W. H. Wiltberger, the Hotel has been leased to Messrs. S. N. Papot & Co. The new proprietors have made many changes and improvements. The whole house has been thoroughly painted, inside and out, and otherwise renovated; and such alterations have been made in the interior arrangements as must add to its attractions and conduce to the comfort of the guests.

At this Hotel every convenience is offered to the traveling public in the way of Ticket Office for the Rail Roads and Steamboats, and here, also, Sleeping Car Tickets can be procured.

The table is furnished with the best meats, poultry and game to be produced in the New York and Baltimore markets, and our corps of cooks is unsurpassed by any in the the country. If kind and courteous treatment, with comfortable rooms, which cannot be excelled, offer any inducements to our friends going South, either for health or pleasure, we think we can safely recommend them to patronize the Pulaski during their sojourn in Savannah.

Marshall House,

SAVANNAH GA.,

A. B. LUCE, Proprietor.

———••———

This is a capital House for Tourists
and Invalids who desire to stay over a
day or two in Savannah. Its table is
excellent, and the rates reasonable, the
price of board being

$3.00 Per Day.

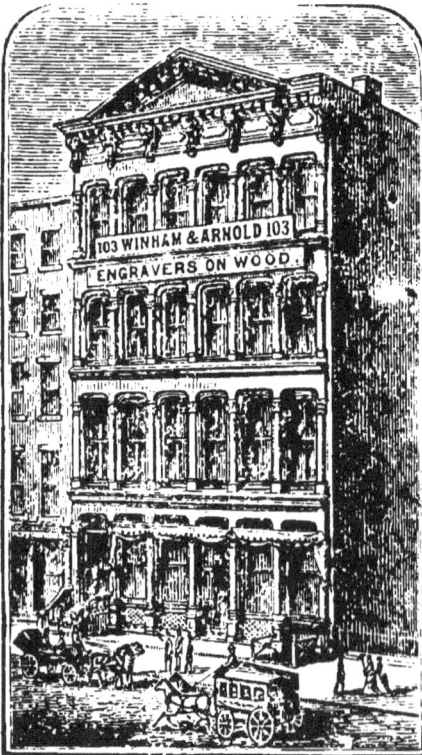

LIEBIG'S EXTRACT OF BEEF,

MONTEVIDEO. •

Manufactured by

Lucas Herrera & Co.

MANUFACTORY IN SOUTH AMERICA: MONTEVIDEO, URUGUAY.

The Extract of Beef, manufactured by Messrs. LUCAS HERRERA & Co., having been examined by Dr. Augustus Voelcker, F. R. S., Consulting Chemist to the Royal Agricultural Society of England, V. Kletzinsky, Professor of Chemistry and Pathology of the Imperial House of Vienna, Dr. E. Reichardt, Professor of the University of Jena, and other celebrated Chemists in Europe, has been recognized as an article of superior quality; and in regard to its purity and flavor is equal to any Extract offered to the trade, according to the improved process of Baron von Liebig.

The improved machinery employed by Messrs. LUCAS HERRERA & Co., the judicious and economical administration of their establishment, together with the facilities afforded by its unequaled position (only twenty-four miles from Montevideo), and the vast pastures and extensive herds of cattle always ready for the exclusive use of the factory, enable the owners of this important establishment to offer their Extracts at extremely low prices, while at the same time a wholesome and superior article is guaranteed.

This Extract—containing as it does, in a concentrated form, the juices of the meat—combines all the elements of a very nutritious food. For every pound of Extract thirty-four pounds of good butcher's beef are required exclusive of bones and fat.

This Extract of Beef is free from fat and gelatine, and is indispensable to every household; it is specially recommended for Military and Naval purposes, for Hospitals and Workhouses, and has been found a very useful article of food during sea voyages.

Independently of an economy of fifty per cent., as compared with butcher's meat, this Extract imparts to soups, ragouts and vegetables of every kind, the strength and savor of the best broths, rendering every dish richer and more palatable.

For Invalids, Convalescents, and children of weak constitutions, it will be found an inestimable article.

Excellent soup can be made by dissolving a tea-spoonful of this Extract in a cupful of hot water, adding sufficient salt, and a little butter if required.

This Extract is sent to England in bulk, and is carefully put into jars of required sizes, by means of improved apparatus.

SOLE AGENTS FOR THE UNITED STATES,

W. H. Schieffelin & Co.,

170 & 172 William Street, N. Y.

www.ingramcontent.com/pod-product-compliance
Lightning Source LLC
Chambersburg PA
CBHW030717110426

42739CB00030B/718